DID YOU KNOW?

TRAINS CAN FLOAT

and other fun facts

D1441623

For Nathaniel
—L. D.

For Michael and Juliette
—H. E.

For Mom and Dad
—P. O.

For Lydia and Jackie Raye
—A. S.

LITTLE SIMON
An imprint of Simon & Schuster Children's Publishing Division
1230 Avenue of the Americas, New York, New York 10020
Series concept by Laura Lyn DiSiena
Copyright © 2014 by Simon & Schuster, Inc.
All rights reserved, including the right of reproduction in whole or in part in any form.
LITTLE SIMON is a registered trademark of Simon & Schuster, Inc., and associated colophon is a trademark of Simon & Schuster, Inc.
For information about special discounts for bulk purchases, please contact Simon & Schuster Special Sales at 1-866-506-1949 or
business@simonandschuster.com. The Simon & Schuster Speakers Bureau can bring authors to your live event. For more information or to book an event
contact the Simon & Schuster Speakers Bureau at 1-866-248-3049 or visit our website at www.simonspeakers.com.
Manufactured in China 0814 SCP
10 9 8 7 6 5 4 3 2
Library of Congress Cataloging-in-Publication Data
DiSiena, Laura Lyn, author.
Trains can float : and other fun facts / by Laura Lyn DiSiena and Hannah Eliot ; illustrated by Pete Oswald. — First edition. pages cm. — (Did you know?)
Summary: "A book of fun facts about all sorts of vehicles and transportation"—Provided by publisher.
Audience: 4-8. Audience: K-3. Includes bibliographical references and index.
ISBN 978-1-4814-0280-4 (pbk) — ISBN 978-1-4814-0281-1 (hc) — ISBN 978-1-4814-0282-8 (ebook) 1. Transportation—Miscellanea—Juvenile literature. 2. Railroad trains—Miscellanea—Juvenile literature.
I. Eliot, Hannah, author. II. Oswald, Pete, illustrator. III. Title.
TA1149.D57 2014   629.04'6—dc23   2013030194

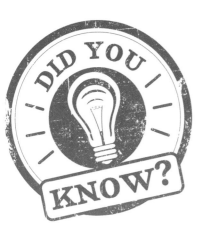
DID YOU KNOW?

TRAINS CAN FLOAT
and other fun facts

By Laura Lyn DiSiena and Hannah Eliot
Illustrated by Pete Oswald
and Aaron Spurgeon

LITTLE SIMON
New York   London   Toronto   Sydney   New Delhi

HEY THERE!

Where are you right now? At home? In the car? Or maybe . . . on a train?
Did you know that the first steam engine train rode the tracks in 1804?
How about that it can take more than a mile for a train to come to a full stop?
Or that the first railway in the world to go to the top of an active volcano was on Mount Vesuvius in Italy?
Okay, okay. Maybe you knew those things. But did you know that trains can FLOAT?

Well, they don't float the way you might imagine. They can't float on *water*. But for certain trains, magnets are used to make the train rise above the tracks, giving it extra speed! These trains are called Maglev trains, and they can go up to 360 miles per hour!

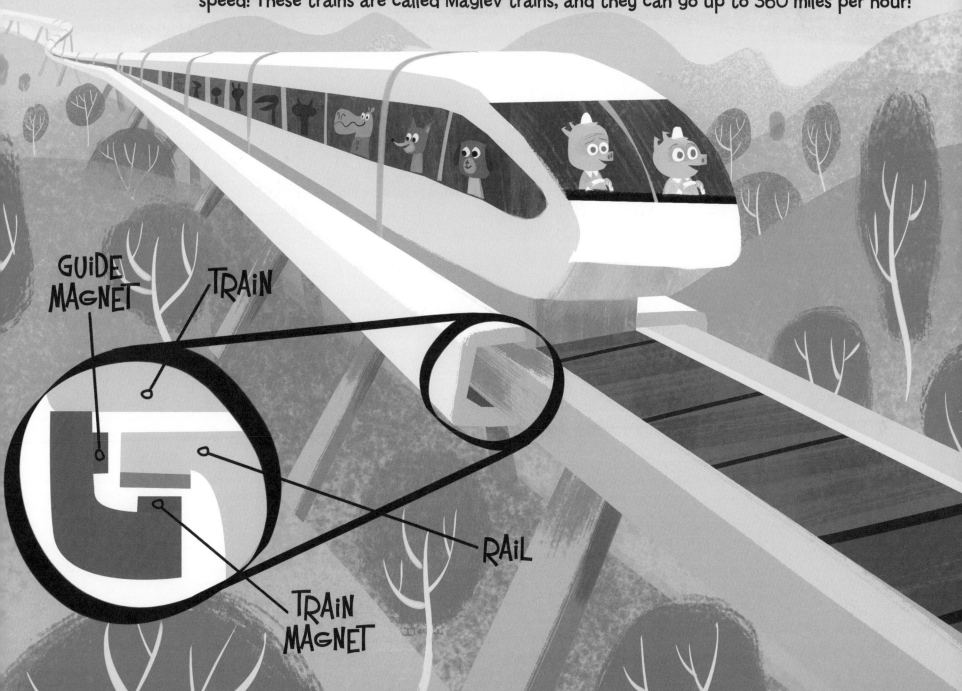

GUIDE MAGNET

TRAIN

RAIL

TRAIN MAGNET

CHOO! CHOO!

Did you know that some trains run through tunnels under city streets? That's right! These are part of what's known as a metro system. There are 188 metro systems in the world. The London Underground is the oldest one. It opened in 1863.

The New York City subway is one one of the world's oldest systems. It's also one of the most crowded! More than 5 million passengers ride the New York City subway each weekday!

Though that's not nearly as crowded as the Tokyo subway—about 9 million passengers ride that one per day!

Did you know that the world's most northern metro system is the Helsinki Metro in Finland?

HELSINKI

★ BUENOS
AIRES

The most southern one is the Buenos Aires Underground!

Taking the metro can be a great way to get to work or school, but if you want to go far away from home, you might travel on an airplane. An airplane can cruise along at more than 500 miles per hour 35,000 feet above Earth!

Some planes are SUPERSONIC. This means they can fly faster than the speed of sound. Now that's fast! These planes are used mostly by the military, but the Concorde (1976-2003) was a supersonic commercial plane used to fly passengers across the Atlantic Ocean. At a speed of more than 1,000 miles per hour, the flight from London to New York was less than 3 and a half hours long. A regular flight takes about 8 hours!

Can you think of another way to fly over the Atlantic Ocean? No, you couldn't ride a bird across, silly! How about a hot-air balloon? People have been riding in hot-air balloons since the late 1700s. In 1978 the first hot-air balloon crossed the Atlantic Ocean, and it took 137 hours, which is almost six days! That sure is SLOW.

Did you know that there are actually hot-air balloon *festivals*?
The largest festival in the world takes place in Albuquerque, New Mexico.
More than 700 balloons launch into the air. Some balloons are even
shaped like houses, dragons, cakes, and more!

What if you wanted to travel UNDER a body of water instead of flying over it? Well, that's what tunnels are for. Tunnels can be built underground, and they can also be built underwater for trains and cars to travel through.

Tunnels are created by a process called EXCAVATION. A combination of manual labor, explosives, and machinery is used to scoop out the dirt and create a space where the tunnel can be built. Have you ever heard about the tunnels in the Netherlands? Well, there are a lot of them, and they're used in a very special way. More than 600 wildlife crossings—paths *over* tunnels—were built to help protect the endangered European badger, plus deer and wild boar, by giving them shelter as well as a way to cross the road!

BEEP! BEEP!

Tunnels are not the only way cars can get between two places separated by water.
Don't forget about bridges! There are many different types of bridges. The Golden Gate Bridge
in San Francisco is a suspension bridge, which means it is supported by cables.
Do you know what color the Golden Gate Bridge is? Not gold . . . oRANGE!
The bold color was chosen so the bridge can be seen through very thick fog.

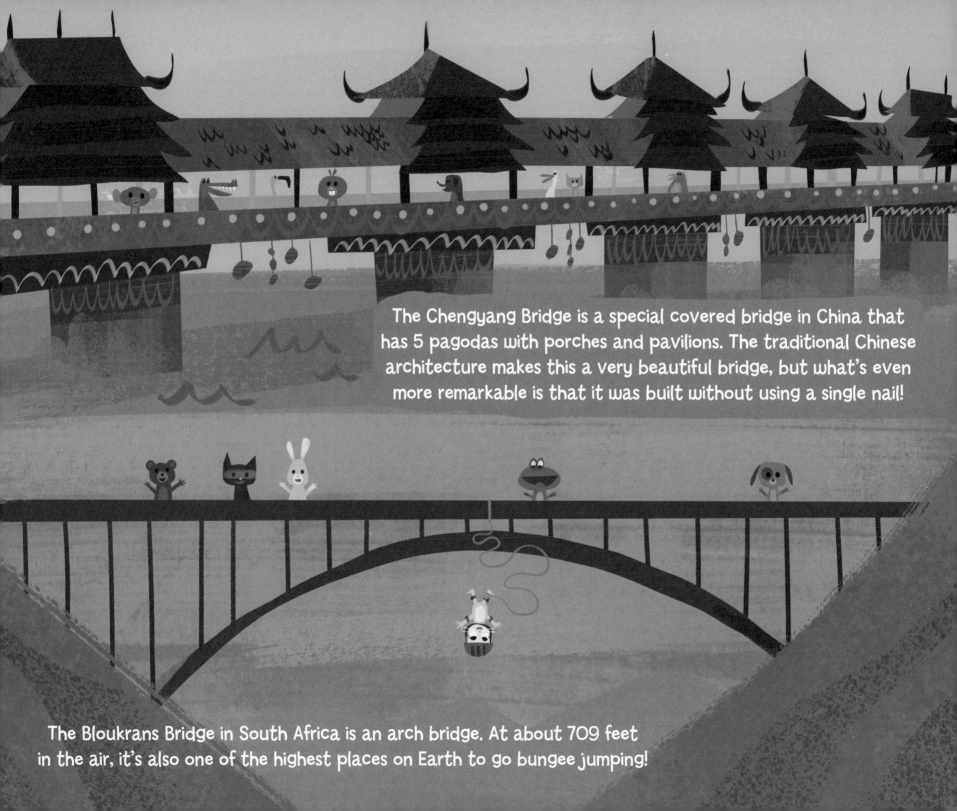

The Chengyang Bridge is a special covered bridge in China that has 5 pagodas with porches and pavilions. The traditional Chinese architecture makes this a very beautiful bridge, but what's even more remarkable is that it was built without using a single nail!

The Bloukrans Bridge in South Africa is an arch bridge. At about 709 feet in the air, it's also one of the highest places on Earth to go bungee jumping!

Bridges have been around since ancient times. The Romans built bridges out of stone and concrete for pedestrians and cargo traffic. Something that's *not* so ancient is the helicopter. Can you think of another name for a helicopter? That's right, a CHOPPER!

A helicopter has rotating blades that are always moving so it can fly up and down, backward and forward, right and left, AND hover in place. Kind of like a hummingbird—except a helicopter has a pilot. The pilot has to constantly operate the controls with both arms and both legs to keep the helicopter in the air. Helicopters are a very important part of firefighting and rescues, and even observing animals in the wild, because they can fly into tight places and get close to the ground.

Helicopters are great for ground missions, but if you're going on a space mission, you're going to need a rocket-powered spacecraft! The power of a rocket engine can propel a spacecraft into Earth's orbit and beyond. In 1969, the *Apollo 11* landed on the moon. That's the farthest into space any one has ever been.

The International Space Station is a spacecraft that has been orbiting Earth since 1998. This spacecraft is also a home and science lab where astronauts can live, go for space walks outside the station, and do research so that eventually we can travel deeper into space than ever before!

Spacecrafts aren't the only rocket-powered vehicles around. Rocket cars are used to compete in drag races. At one point, a rocket car called *Blue Flame* held the record for fastest land speed. The car went 622 miles per hour!

There are many types of cars. Some cars run on electricity. And some cars run without any engine at all—such as soapbox cars and some go-carts! Soapbox cars are called this because they used to be made out of wooden soap crates, with roller-skate wheels attached. These days they are a little more high-tech, and they're known as gravity racers. In a race, the cars usually start at the top of a hill and GRAVITY powers them to the finish line. Buckle those seat belts and helmets!

It's a good idea to wear your helmet when riding your bike, too. Can you think of a reason why a bicycle is such a great choice for transportation? How about . . . bikes don't cause pollution! Plus they're not very expensive compared to cars. And not only does riding a bike get you where you want to go, it's also fun and good exercise! Those are some GREAT reasons!

A unicycle is a bicycle, but with only one wheel. Have you ever been to the circus? Well, you've probably seen one there. Maybe a clown was riding it! You probably also saw trapeze artists (Hey, that's one way to get from one side of the room to the other!) and performers on stilts (another way to get where you're going)!

Something you might see at the circus—but more likely on the sidewalk—is a skateboard. It is thought that skateboarding probably started in the 1940s in California because surfers wanted something to "surf" when the waves were flat. Since they take a lot of energy to ride, most people use skateboards for short distances. Can you imagine taking one TRANSCONTINENTAL?

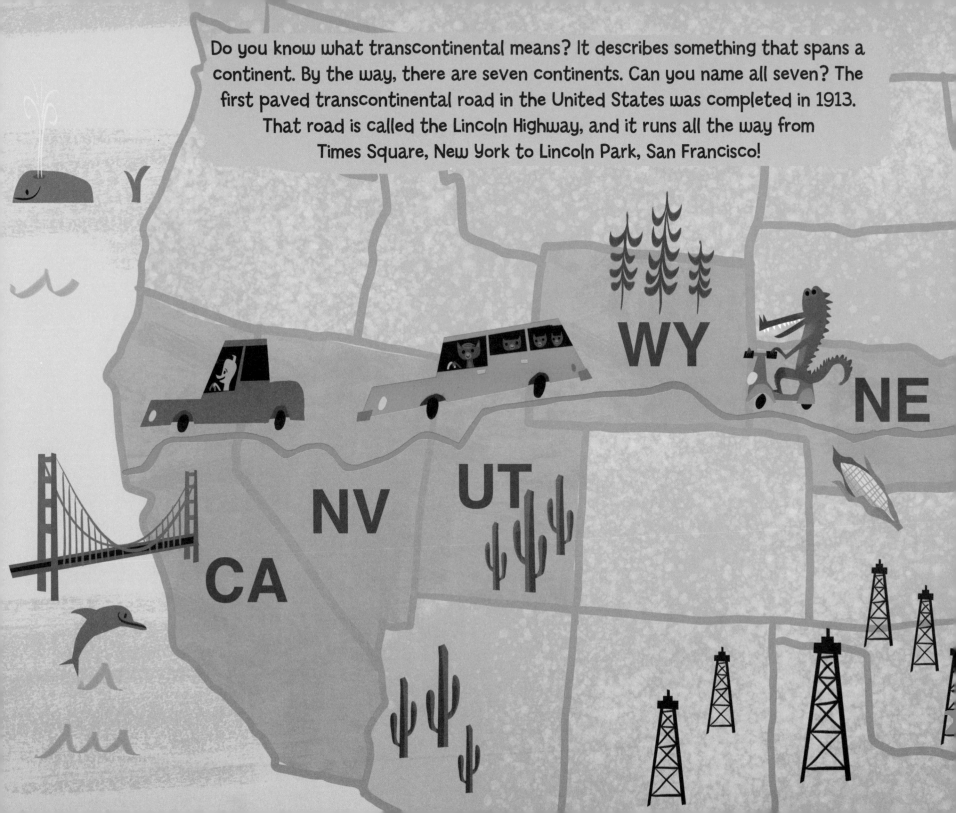

Do you know what transcontinental means? It describes something that spans a continent. By the way, there are seven continents. Can you name all seven? The first paved transcontinental road in the United States was completed in 1913. That road is called the Lincoln Highway, and it runs all the way from Times Square, New York to Lincoln Park, San Francisco!

If you are in San Francisco, you can visit the USS *Pampanito*, a submarine from World War II. The word submarine means "under the sea." Submarines are boats that function underwater, sometimes for months at a time. A submarine will float on top of the water when its ballast tanks are full of air, and when it's time to sink down into the water, these tanks release the air and get filled with water. Submarines can go deeper into the ocean than divers, so scientists use submarines to study marine life and explore the ocean floor.

Most boats float *on top* of water rather than being submerged *in the* water!
Do you know the difference between boats and ships?
A boat is a vessel small enough to be carried aboard another vessel—such as a ship!

Many boats and ships have engines, which make them able travel very fast. The world's fastest speedboat has 4 engines and can go 250 miles per hour! That's faster than a lot of trains can go. And unlike a *train* in water, boats sure can FLOAT!

MORE FUN FACTS

Metro system: From 1904-1948, a ticket to ride the New York City subway only cost 5 cents. Today, the fare costs $2.50!

Airplane: Because of the air pressure, about a third of the taste buds in our mouth actually go numb when we are flying in an airplane. Lots of people order tomato juice when they normally wouldn't because it tastes better to them at 35,000 feet in the air!

Train: Today, 40 percent of the world's freight cargo is transported via trains, and that number keeps growing!

Japan

Hot-air balloon: Hot-air balloons float by using a bag that contains heated air. The hot air makes the balloon buoyant because it is less dense than the cold air around it.

Tunnel: The longest undersea tunnel in the world is the Seikan Tunnel in Japan—it's 14.5 miles!

Bridge: Depending on the temperature, the Sydney Harbour Bridge in Australia can rise or fall up to 7 inches due to its steel expanding or contracting.

Skateboard: The ollie is a skateboarding trick that involves the rider and skateboard leaping into the air at the same time without the rider using his or her hands.

Helicopter: The word "helicopter" comes from the Greek "helix/helikos," meaning "spiral/turning," and "pteron," meaning "wing."

Car: In Sweden a man was fined nearly $1 million for speeding at 180 miles per hour!

Road: The world's oldest known paved road was laid in Egypt some time between 2600 and 2200 BC.

Bicycle: Orville and Wilbur Wright, the brothers who built the first flying airplane, owned a small bike repair shop in Dayton, Ohio. They used that workshop to build the famous Wright Flyer in 1903.

Space shuttle: While it's in orbit, a space shuttle travels around Earth at a speed of about 17,500 miles per hour. At this speed, the passengers on board can see a sunrise or sunset every 45 minutes!

Submarine: As a tribute to the Beatles—who sang the song "Yellow Submarine"—a 51-foot-long yellow metal submarine sculpture was constructed in 1984. It can now be seen at the John Lennon Airport in Liverpool, England.

Boat: There are three categories of boats—human powered or unpowered, sailboats, and motorboats.